Phenom

Marjorie Rose Bernadin

- Rejection
- Depression
- Witchcraft
- Church Hurt
- Heartbreak

PHENOMENALLY SHE ROSE

FROM TRIALS TO TRIUMPHANT

PSALM 46:5 GOD IS WITHIN HER, SHE WILL NOT FALL.

Phenomenally She Rose: *Marjorie Rose Bernadin*

Become an author today!

Soar Book Publishing
www.Soarbookpublishing@yahoo.com

🌷 *Phenomenally She Rose* 🌷

From: Trials to Triumphant
By: Marjorie Rose Bernadin

All rights reserved. No portion of this book may be produced, stored in a retrieval system, or transmitted in any form or by any means- electronic, mechanical, photocopy, recording, scanning, or other- except for a brief quotation in critical reviews or articles, without the prior written permission of the publisher.

Unless otherwise noted, Scripture quotations are taken from the New King James Version ®. ©1982 by Thomas Nelson. Used with permission. All rights reserved. Any product, phone number and internet addresses printed in this book are offered as a resource and are not intended to be or to imply an endorsement by Thomas Nelson, nor does Thomas Nelson vouch for the existence, content, or products beyond the life of this book. 🌷🌷🌷🌷🌷🌷🌷🌷🌷

2023 Marjorie Rose Bernadin
ISBN: 979-8-9884331-0-1

🌷 **Publisher information:** Soar Book Publishing LLC
🌷 **Publisher information:** soarbookpublishing@yahoo.com
Photo Credit: **Marjorie Rose Bernadin**

Phenomenally She Rose: *Marjorie Rose Bernadin*

🌷 *Dedication* 🌷

To every woman that is determined to RISE from rejection, abuse, heartbreak, low self-esteem, church hurt, mental disorders and witchcraft through Christ JESUS... this one is for us.

Phenomenally She ROSE 🌷

Phenomenally She Rose: *Marjorie Rose Bernadin*

🌹 *Acknowledgements* 🌹

    I would first like to honor and reverence to GOD. I am thankful to GOD for HIS grace and mercy. I am thankful that GOD never abandoned me when I was at my worst. I am who I am today because of GOD's sovereignty, faithfulness, and unfailing love. Despite all that I have been through, GOD has equipped me to love, hope, overcome and flourish into a Phenomenal ROSE.

    I would like to thank my father and mother for their sacrifice and love towards me. As I age in grace, I understand that my parents did the very best that they could for me. For that, I am grateful.

    I would like to thank family members, friends and spiritual leaders who have stood by me along this journey of healing to encourage me, pray for me, support me, and help me to birth the vision that GOD placed within.

    I would like to thank my spiritual leaders, Apostle Bruner Remy and Prophetess Cathy N. Remy for their prayers, biblical teachings, and support along my spiritual process.

    Lastly, I would like to thank Soar Book Publishing. Thank you for giving life to my vision. Thank you for providing excellent customer service, organization, and creativity. It was an honor working with your company to help publish my very first book. 🌹 🌹 🌹 🌹 🌹 🌹 🌹 🌹 🌹 🌹 🌹 🌹

Phenomenally She Rose: *Marjorie Rose Bernadin*

Table of Contents

🌷 **Dedications**

🌷 **Acknowledgments**

Chapter 1 🌷 She *ROSE* from Rejection………………2

Chapter 2 🌷 She *ROSE* from Heartbreak…………….10

Chapter 3 🌷 She *ROSE* from Low Self-esteem………19

Chapter 4 🌷 She *ROSE* from Church Hurt…………...29

Chapter 5 🌷 She *ROSE* from Depression…………….39

Chapter 6 🌷 She *ROSE* from Witchcraft…………….48

Chapter 7 🌷 She *ROSE* from Death………………….58

🌷 **About the Author……………………….. 67**

🌷 **Marjorie Rose Celebration……………...68**

🌷 **Mental Health Resources………………..72**

Phenomenally She Rose: *Marjorie Rose Bernadin*

Chapter 1:

She *ROSE* from **Rejection**

"When my father and my mother forsake me,
Then the LORD will take care of me"
- Psalm 27:10

Phenomenally She Rose: *Marjorie Rose Bernadin*

POEM: A Blooming *Rose* 🌹
Written by: Marjorie Rose Bernadin

*She **ROSE**, born into an imperfect world. Her generational roots played a major impact on who she would sprout to become.*

*She **ROSE** into poorly drained soil, unprepared to receive such a gift of life.*

No one noticed the delicate flower from within, swaddled in roots of rejection.

*She **ROSE** from a life of unpredictable wind patterns rooted deep in instability, depression, and loneliness.*

Amid poor-quality soil, she bloomed.
Within extreme climate changes, she bloomed.
Her leaves broken, yet vibrant, she bloomed.
Generational roots of rejection attempted to stunt her growth with its blackspot and mildew.

*Against all odds, with a bit of sunlight **LOVE** and fertilized **HOPE**, she **Bloomed**.*

Phenomenally She Rose: *Marjorie Rose Bernadin*

"You are divinely LOVED and ACCEPTED by GOD, and that is enough"
-*Marjorie Rose Bernadin*

A father's love is the greatest asset to a child's personal development. A rejected child may become an unbalanced adult. A loved child may become a wholesome adult. As a child, I battled with Rejection. Rejection of a father. Rejection of family. Rejection of society. All I have ever wanted was my father's unconditional love. I did everything possible to make him proud of me. I sought good grades and awards, and followed the rules; however, nothing that I'd done measured up. I never received a hug or affection. I was never affirmed of my beauty and goodness. I never heard him say, "I Love You".

The more that I sought my father's love, the more that I experienced pain. My childhood was plagued with rejection. My siblings and I also experienced physical and verbal abuse. In public, we were as the perfect blended Christian family. My father was a successful businessman, and my mother was a stay-at-home wife who would work part-time occasionally. But, within the closed walls stood rage, power, and abuse. With physical abuse, bruises eventually heal. With verbal and psychological abuse, the words never leave your soul. As a child, I witnessed one of my siblings attempt suicide due to the abuse. As a teen, I also attempted suicide. Rejection led me to believe that I was not worthy of love.

In my 20s while searching for my birth certificate to apply for a passport, I discovered that I had two different birth certificates. Each birth certificate was a few years apart. When asked why? I was told that it was because my father didn't want me. I cried and didn't eat for three whole days. I grew up experiencing a daily rejection, because the one who raised me didn't want me. In my quest for love, it left me bankrupt.

I unreasonably experienced rejection of siblings, classmates, and society. I had a difficult time with fitting in. Girls didn't like me because I was tall, curvy, intelligent, and pretty. I tried to fit in during middle and high school by: people pleasing, starving myself to be thinner, and dimming my academic brightness. In avoiding rejection of others, I had learned to reject myself.

> *I had a difficult time with fitting in. Girls didn't like me because I was tall, curvy, intelligent, and pretty.*

How did "REJECTION" affect my life?

The markings of rejection have affected my life: physically, psychologically, emotionally, relationally, and spiritually. Rejection led to years of depression, anxiety, and low self-esteem. I felt unwanted, undeserving, unloved, and hopeless. I had several suicidal attempts. I sought love and validation from the wrong type of men. I avoided people, places, and opportunities that required intimacy. I lived a lifestyle of perfectionism, avoiding making any mistakes. I also had a difficult time with accepting the love of GOD. For years, I compared GOD to my earthly father and would hide from GOD each time I sinned, because I felt unworthy. My earthly father exemplified conditional love, for it was based on my performance; therefore, why would a PERFECT GOD love an imperfect and flawed me?

Rejection plagued my life, till the day I decided to accept GOD's unconditional love for me.

How did I RISE from Rejection?

The antidote to Rejection is **ACCEPTANCE.**

I had to accept that GOD's love was enough. I needed to believe that GOD loves me unconditionally. GOD's relentless love pursued after me without fail. No matter my mistakes, flaws, sinful nature, or shortcomings, GOD never stopped loving me. Although family, classmates and so many others rejected me, GOD never rejected me. I became free, once I believed by faith that nothing could separate me from the love of GOD. Through Christ Jesus, I Phenomenally *ROSE* from rejection into *Acceptance* of love. GOD is Love.

🌹 ENCOURAGEMENT 🌹

To everyone who has ever battled with rejection of a father, mother, siblings, peers, lovers, society, and self. To you, I say, GOD loves you. You are loved just as you are. Your earthly parents may not have planned you, but you are NOT a mistake or unforeseen phenomena to GOD. You are loved by the creator of the universe, and nothing can separate you from the love of JESUS Christ. You are loved, accepted, and welcomed into a Kingdom family. It's time to accept GOD's love and forgive those who rejected you. You must forgive yourself and release the pain of yesterday. May you RISE from rejection into a place of *Acceptance* through Christ Jesus.

AFFIRMATION:
1. I am divinely Loved and Accepted by GOD.
2. I am good enough the way that I am.
3. Rejection does not define me.

Bible verses to help **OVERCOME** Rejection:
1. "When my father and my mother forsake me, Then the LORD will take care of me." (Psalm 27:10)
2. "Yet in all these things we are more than conquerors through Him who loved us. For I am persuaded that neither death nor life, nor angels nor principalities nor powers, nor things present nor things to come, nor height nor depth, nor any other created thing, shall be able to separate us from the love of GOD which is in Christ Jesus our Lord." (Romans 8: 37-39)
3. "For the LORD will not cast off His people, nor will He forsake His inheritance." (Psalm 94: 14)
4. "For I know the thoughts that I think toward you, says the LORD, thoughts of peace and not of evil, to give you a future and a hope." (Jeremiah 29:11)

PRAYER:

Dear: Heavenly Father,
I come before your throne of grace to ask for your forgiveness of sins. I ask for your help to forgive those who have sinned against me. Father GOD, help me to forgive those who has rejected me, abandoned me, neglected me, and abused me in any capacity. I pray that through the help of the Holy Spirit that I may accept your unconditional

love. May I truly believe in my heart that neither death nor life, angels nor rulers, things present nor things to come, nor powers, nor height nor depth, nor anything else in all creation will be able to separate me from your love (Romans 8: 37-39). May I RISE this day from rejection into full *Acceptance* of your unconditional love for me, in JESUS mighty name I pray, amen.

Phenomenally She Rose: *Marjorie Rose Bernadin*

Chapter 2:

She *ROSE* from Heartbreak

"The LORD is near to those who have a broken heart, and saves such as have a contrite spirit"
- Psalm 34:18

Phenomenally She Rose: *Marjorie Rose Bernadin*

POEM: A *Rose* of New Beginnings 🌹
Written by: Marjorie Rose Bernadin

One rose of love at first sight.
Two roses of affection.
Three roses of passion.
A fourth rose arose jealousy within.
The fifth rose led to infidelity.
What began as a lovely ROSE,
Has now left traces of broken pedals.

A sixth rose has died.
A seventh rose conjured a season of deadheading,
The process of removal of all dead things.
An eighth rose has now blossomed into NEW Beginnings.

Phenomenally She Rose: *Marjorie Rose Bernadin*

"The purest ESSENCE of Love is GOD"
-Marjorie Rose Bernadin

To experience LOVE is the highest quest, for GOD is LOVE (1 John 4:7-8). Before sin came to be, GOD created Adam and Eve in a state of plenty and fashioned them into the wholeness of HIS love. Before sin, Adam and Eve lived a prosperous life in GOD's Garden. Adam was given Eve, the bone of his bone, and flesh of his flesh. In the presence of Love, they were unaware of each other's nakedness (Genesis 2: 8-25). To be loved wholeheartedly by someone special is the closest thing to the garden of Eden; however, sin brought a curse into humanity, and it introduced Brokenness. The first Adam removed humanity from the deity of Love and lost his identity. The second Adam (JESUS Christ) restored humanity back to LOVE (1 Corinthians 15:21-49). Brokenness led me to search for love in all the wrong places. In the purest essence of Love, I ROSE from Heartbreak back to Love.

During my freshman year in high school, I was involved in a relationship with a young man. He was a few years older than I. We ended our relationship 9 months later because my parents were very strict, and I was not allowed to go out much. During my senior year, we reconnected and decided to give the relationship another try. I thought at 17 years of age that I was madly in love. I had never experienced the unconditional love of a father, so this relationship filled the void that I was seeking. This guy was my first love. I thought we were

> *The first Adam removed humanity from the deity of Love and lost his identity. The second Adam (JESUS Christ) restored humanity back to LOVE.*

inseparable; however, before my high school graduation, my world as I remembered it came crumbling down. My mother disapproved of my relationship and did everything possible to end it. I remember her phoning the elders of the church, asking for a meeting. My parents then gave me an ultimatum to end the relationship or leave their house. Me and the young man decided to temporarily end the relationship, in hopes that we would be together after I turned 18. Approximatively 3 weeks later, I graduated from High School and celebrated my 18th birthday. It was a very difficult season for me because my parents were upset with me, they involved the church, my father did not attend my High School graduation and I was forced to end my relationship. It was at my 18th birthday party that I had discovered that this young man, whom I thought I was madly in love with, was married to another woman. He married her within 3 weeks of us breaking up and invited his wife to my 18th birthday block party. My heart was shattered into pieces. I had experienced Rejection of a father and now, I was experiencing Heartbreak from my first love.

How did "Heartbreak" affect my life?

Broken heartedness led me through a season of bitterness. I felt so humiliated publicly, shamed, rejected and heart broken. I felt rejected by my father and now men. I witnessed how men mistreated women, and I vowed to myself that I would never let any man hurt me like that again. That experience changed the trajectory of how I viewed love and relationships. It was engraved in my mind that love equates to pain, therefore love is not desirable. I would spend the next 10 years of my life bitter.

Phenomenally She Rose: *Marjorie Rose Bernadin*

My heart grew cold. I had one agenda and that was to make men pay at all costs. I was hurting men who had nothing to do with my past. I rejected all promising relationships that represented the nature of love. Although I thought I had the upper hand, the one person who was losing was myself because I was consumed with unforgiveness.

> *My heart grew cold. I had one agenda and that was to make men pay at all costs. I was hurting men who had nothing to do with my past. I rejected all promising relationships that represented the nature of love.*

When your heart is impure, it opens the door to impure spirits. My heart became impure through rejection and heartbreak. An impure heart opened the door to the spirit of perversion and identity confusion. Since I was hurt by men, I began to experience same sex attraction. Although, I never physically dated a woman, I would watch same sex porn, masturbate, and desire women. The devil wanted me to believe that the reason it wasn't working out with men, is because I needed to be with a woman. I also became addicted to pornography. No longer did I desire men as much sexually because I was able to satisfy myself. Through the seed of rejection, roots of lust and perversion sprouted in my garden.

How did I RISE from Heartbreak?

The antidote to Heartbreak is *Love.*

One day, I woke up and realized that I had spent over 10 years bitter, confused, broken, living in sin and still single. GOD led me to a ministry that preached heavily on love and waiting till marriage. True love waits. For the first time in my life, that I no longer wanted to watch porn, masturbate, or fornicate. I desired holiness and real love. Breaking free from the spirit of perversion is not easy. My deliverance required the help of the Holy Spirit, and a lifestyle of prayer, fasting and consecration. There are times that I fell into sin and had to repent. But I never gave up on pursuing Holiness & Purity. During my deliverance, I also had to forgive myself, forgive my father and forgive the first guy who broke my heart. When I began to forgive and heal properly, my vision and appetite changed. I found myself less interested in watching illicit images and no longer attracted to the same sex. I began pursuing after purity. In the beginning, I thought purity was the absence of sexual sin. HOLY SPIRIT began to reveal to me that purity is the way of keeping your mind, heart, and body from being tainted (2 Timothy 2:22). Broken heartedness led to years of bitterness and a lifestyle of sin. When I gave my brokenness to JESUS, He traded my sinfulness for HIS righteousness and filled my heart with HIS love. Through Christ JESUS, I Phenomenally *ROSE* from Heartbreak back into *Love.*

🌹 ENCOURAGEMENT 🌹

GOD has a plan for your life. GOD has thoughts to prosper you and not to harm you. Thoughts to give you a future with an expected end. Just because someone doesn't see your value, doesn't mean you don't have any value. GOD loves you and have a wonderful plan for your life. If you desire true freedom, you must choose to forgive and let go. You must forgive everyone who has ever hurt you. When you harbor pain, you give room for bitterness, sickness, curses, and perversion to manifest in your life. Hurt people hurt people. When you choose not to forgive you begin to hurt innocent people and push good people away. When you choose not to forgive, you will not be forgiven by GOD. We must extend forgiveness to receive forgiveness. Forgiveness does not mean re-entry back to your life, but it does mean that your heart is free from hate. Forgiveness will set you free. May you ***RISE*** from Heartbreak back to Love.

AFFIRMATIONS:
1. The Love of Christ JESUS heals my Broken heart.
2. I am worthy of Love.
3. I forgive my ex and all those who broke my heart.

Bible verses to help **OVERCOME** Heartbreak:
1. "The LORD is near to those who have a broken heart, and saves such as have a contrite spirit." (Psalm 34:18)
2. "He heals the brokenhearted and binds up their wounds."

    (Psalm 147:3)
3. Beloved, let us love one another: for love is of God; and everyone that Loves is born of God and knows God. He who does not love does not know God, for God is Love. (1 John 4:7-8)
4. "For if you forgive men their trespasses, your heavenly Father will also forgive you. But if you do not forgive men their trespasses, neither will your Father forgive your trespasses." (Matthew 6:14-15)

PRAYER:

Dear: Heavenly Father,

I come before your throne of grace, and I ask for your forgiveness of sins. I also ask for your help to forgive those who have broken my heart. You said in your words that if I do not forgive others their sins, you will not forgive me of my sins. I asked for your help, through the Holy Spirit to forgive, as you have forgiven me. Help me to release the pain of heartbreak and to forgive as many times as possible. Create in me a clean heart and renew your right spirit within me. May your LOVE saturate my heart to receive and give love freely. May I RISE this day from Heartbreak into LOVE, in JESUS mighty name, I pray, amen.

Phenomenally She Rose: *Marjorie Rose Bernadin*

Chapter 3:

She *ROSE* from *Low Self-Esteem*

"I will praise You, for I am fearfully and wonderfully made, marvelous are Your works, and that my soul knows very well." - Psalm 139:14

POEM: Set *Free* by Love 🌷
Written by: Marjorie Rose Bernadin

I was once terrified of love.
Terrified that love would not love me.
Terrified that my love may not have been good enough, strong enough, wise enough, faithful enough, tender enough or sweet enough to stay.

Good enough, to decrease the competition to none.
Wise enough, to know if what I felt was true.
Faithful enough to commit to one's body, mind, and soul.
Strong enough to endure all the trials and tribulations that would stand in the way.

I was once terrified of love.
Terrified that I might have said or done the wrong things.
Terrified that I wouldn't be pretty enough, smart enough, thin enough, curvy enough, soft enough, or woman enough to be loved.

Terrified that with love, I'd only be wasting my time.
Placed back on the market after being depreciated.
Left with only heartaches and pain.
Terrified that love would hurt more than it will heal.
Terrified that love would have left me bankrupt.

Until one encounter with LOVE restored me.
LOVE entered my heart and removed the heart of stone and Gave me a heart of flesh.

Phenomenally She Rose: *Marjorie Rose Bernadin*

LOVE transformed me and gave me a new Identity.
LOVE washed me with tender mercies.
LOVE became my Lord, Redeemer, Healer,
Way Maker, Provider, Protector, and Friend.
LOVE broke through all my fears and barriers.

I was once terrified of love,
That I couldn't receive or provide love.
Until one encounter with JESUS Christ set me free.
GOD is Love.
I am set free by LOVE.

Phenomenally She Rose: *Marjorie Rose Bernadin*

"I was created FLAWLESS by a Perfect GOD"
-Marjorie Rose Bernadin

Self-esteem is measured from the lens it is viewed. When self-esteem is tainted by rejection, it leads to a negative response of low self-worth. During my sophomore year in college, I had decided to give love another chance; however, the guy that I liked told me that he saw me as only a friend. Rejected once more, led to years of low self-esteem. I felt that I was not good enough, pretty enough, smart enough, worthy enough, nor fair-skinned to be loved. From that moment, I dated random men for validation. I would jump from relationship to relationship seeking for men to affirm me, accept me, and love me. I rejected and disqualified myself from the possibility of something good. I tolerated toxic relationships because that's what I felt that I deserved. Lack of self-worth led me to exchange abuse for love. Because I didn't love myself, I was attracted to men who didn't love neither. I attracted men who were narcissistic, abusive, manipulative, addicted to substance, and had low self-esteem. I attracted men who had no ambition and were emotionally unavailable. The way that I allowed men to treat me reflected how I viewed myself. My lens was distorted.

> *I tolerated toxic relationships because that's what I felt that I deserved. Lack of self-worth led me to exchange abuse for love.*

During college, I had developed this mindset that bad attention was better than no attention. I dated an older guy who was verbally and psychologically abusive. He told me that I was unattractive and that no one would ever love or want someone like me. While having sex, he looked me in the eyes and told me, "If only you had surgery on your entire face than maybe you would be desirable." I knew I had reached a low point in my life, when he called another woman to meet him at his place, while I was in the car, dropping him off to the airport. As a child, I witnessed my mother being mistreated and verbally abused and now I was repeating the same vicious cycle. When I tried to end the relationship, he threatened me. I remembered being in my college apartment, contemplating suicide because I honestly believed that death was the only way that would free me from him. It was at that moment, I prayed and cried out to JESUS for help. I also reached out to one of my sisters for prayer. A few weeks after, he completely left me alone and moved on to another woman. After that breakup, I found myself in multiple trauma bonding relationships that I confused for love. I began dating international men, hoping that I would find better luck in love. I traveled internationally in pursuit of love and validation, only to realize that I was still attracting broken men. The problem wasn't the men I was dating, it was me. I was the common denominator.

How did "Low Self-esteem" affect my life?

Low self-worth led to a life of self-rejection. In my 20s, I would never purchase anything of value for myself because I didn't believe that I deserved it. I would receive expensive gifts from others, but I would not purchase anything expensive or valuable for me. In each store that I shopped, I gravitated towards the "**CLEARANCE**" section. I wouldn't buy any shirts that cost more than $5 or pants more than $10- $15. Low self-worth led me through a season of attracting people, places, and things of lessor value. I reached one of my lowest seasons in adulthood. I was tired of the toxic relationships and feeling used by men. One day, I heard GOD say to me, "Stop letting men treat you and use you like you are from a clearance rack. Nothing about you will ever be used again." Those words pierced my soul; yet those very words saved my life. In the clearance rack, you find used and devalued items. It is the place where items that were once new are returned with reduced price tags. I was allowing men to use me and devalue me, only to place me back on the shelves when I was no longer marketable. Gradually, I became more conscious of my worth. At the age of 29, is when I truly began my journey of Self-love. I had a brand-new car and a new mindset. I stopped shopping at the clearance rack and stopped entertaining broken men.

How did I RISE from Low Self-esteem?

The antidote to Low Self-esteem is Godly **Confidence.**

GODs relentless love pursued me. Although men became an idol, GOD never stopped loving me. I thought I needed a man to make me whole, but all the while I just needed JESUS. No man was able to fill the emptiness, quench my thirst, or make me whole. When I gave GOD my broken pieces, that is when LOVE entered my heart and GOD began the process of healing. GOD healed me spiritually, mentally, emotionally, physically, and relationally. In the presence of GOD, my confidence was built. It was not an overnight success. To acquire healing and **Confidence** requires Acknowledgement, Accountability, and Intentionality.

Phenomenally She Rose: *Marjorie Rose Bernadin*

Prior to publishing this book, I attended counseling for about two years. Therapy, prayers, affirmations, motivational videos, sermons, journaling, workout regimens and self-care helped me heal and rebuild my self-confidence. I had to forgive every man who has ever hurt me and reject me. I wrote unsent letters to men forgiving them and asking for their forgiveness. I took the initiative for the role that I played in my pain. I had to stop playing the card of victim and learned to see myself as victorious. In my 30s, I dated less.

> *Through Christ Jesus, I overcame low self-worth. I Phenomenally ROSE from Low Self-esteem to a* **Confident** *queen.*

Singleness was a time for me to focus on: loving myself, forgiving myself and dating myself. I also had to unlearn traits and patterns that I had learned from my upbringing. Throughout this healing journey, I cried a lot and released so much pain that I was carrying from birth. I was never in the journey alone; GOD was with me. Whenever it became too hard, the Holy Spirit encouraged me. I also had a support team that consisted of counselors, friends, and spiritual leaders who encouraged me, loved me, and prayed for me throughout the process. Through Christ Jesus, I overcame low self-worth. I Phenomenally ROSE from Low Self-esteem to a **Confident** queen.

🌷 ENCOURAGEMENT 🌷

You are fearfully and wonderfully made. You are a child of the Most High GOD. You are royalty. You are accepted. You are valuable. You are loved. GOD is the potter, and you are the clay; therefore, GOD knows how to put the broken pieces of your life back together again. GOD desires to exchange your ashes for Beauty. You must also spend time in GODs word to renew your mind. You don't need to earn love or validation from people because you are already LOVED and valued by GOD. It doesn't matter what others say or think about you. What matters is what you believe about you. It's time to RISE into the *Confident Queen* that you were created to be, from the beginning.

AFFIRMATIONS:
1. I am fearfully and wonderfully made.
2. I am valuable.
3. I am worthy of Love.

Scriptures to <u>OVERCOME</u> Low Self-esteem:

1. "Do not remember the former things, nor consider the things of old. Behold, I will do a new thing, now it shall spring forth; shall you not know it? I will even make a road in the wilderness and rivers in the desert"
(Isaiah 43: 18-19)
2. "I will praise You, for I am fearfully and wonderfully. Made, marvelous are Your works, and that my soul knows very well." (Psalm 139:14)
3. "She is more precious than rubies, and all the things you may desire cannot compare with her" -Proverbs 3:15

4. "I have loved you with an everlasting love; I have drawn you with unfailing kindness" (Jeremiah 31:3)

PRAYER:

Dear: Heavenly Father,

I come before your throne of grace, and I ask for your forgiveness of sins for all self-rejection and self-hatred. Forgive me for devaluing my worth due to my own distorted view of myself. I asked for your help, through the Holy Spirit to love me the way that you love and see me the way that you see me. Help me to believe that I am fearfully and wonderfully made. Help me to believe that I am more precious than rubies. May your love draw me to you with unfailing kindness. May I RISE this day from Low Self-esteem into Godly *Confidence*, in JESUS mighty name, I pray, amen.

Phenomenally She Rose: *Marjorie Rose Bernadin*

Chapter 4:
She *ROSE* from Church Hurt

"By this all will know that you are My disciples, if you have love for another" - John 13:35

POEM: BRIDE without Blemish 🌹
Written by: Marjorie Rose Bernadin

Lamb of GOD that comes to take away the sins of this world,
May your shed blood have mercy on us this day.
A blemish Bride, not yet ready to be seen by the King.
She is tainted with lies, greed, haughtiness, covetousness, lust, and rebellion.
She judges your people with unfair scales,
She shows partiality to those with wealth,
And discontent to the poor,
She uses her lips to praise you and her tongue to slay your children.
Foolish virgins not yet ready to be seen by their King.

In a world full of darkness,

Her salt has lost its flavor,
Whom you love, she hates,
Whom you hate, she loves,
Preoccupied by the cares of this world,
Her virgin's lamp has ceased to kindle.

Lamb of GOD that comes to take away the sins of this world,
May your shed blood have mercy on us this day.
Purify the heart of your Bride.
Remove her guilty stains.
Seal her with your Holy Spirit.

May your Holy fire set her ablaze, once more.
May she seek what you love,
May she detest what you hate.
May kingdom be her priority, once more.
Light her on the hilltop for your glory.
Wise virgins, with lamps full, ready to be seen by their King.
May the LORD Of lords, and KING of kings find his Bride
Without blemish.

Phenomenally She Rose: *Marjorie Rose Bernadin*

"The CHURCH is as a hospital, where everyone needs a dose of: Hope, Faith, and LOVE"

-*Marjorie Rose Bernadin*

The Church is the Bride of Christ. It is a structure that joins Believers together for fellowship and spiritual growth. The church has also been compared to a hospital that seeks to treat those who are sick. But what happens when the Bride of Christ abuses her authority and begins to mistreat the very people it was sent to deliver? Who will speak for the voiceless? I have experienced Church hurt in many facets. Through faith in Christ JESUS, I Phenomenally *ROSE* from "Church Hurt" into the untainted Bride of Christ.

> *I have experienced Church hurt in many facets. Through faith in Christ JESUS, I Phenomenally ROSE from "Church Hurt" into the untainted Bride of Christ.*

At the age of 17, I experienced my first encounter with Church hurt. I found myself standing before a church committee alongside my parents and my then boyfriend's parents. My mother contacted her local church requesting assistance to end her daughter's relationship. My mother felt that my ex-boyfriend was not a right fit for her daughter. The church committee was set to decide my faith concerning my relationship.

The meeting completely took a turn for the worse. My parents were upset with me, and the committee decided that it's best that me and my then boyfriend, breakup. As a result, my father did not attend my high school graduation. On my 18th birthday, the man that I thought I would spend the rest of my life with, married another woman, just three weeks from our pretend breakup and brought her to my birthday party. That same week, my parents church was having a corporate revival, which involved multiple churches within the Haitian community. My father decided it was best to use this opportunity to discipline me publicly. He walked to the altar and grabbed the microphone to announce to the entire church community that I and my mother were no good, that I never invited him to my high school graduation and that my mother was not a good wife. I remember in that moment of shame, that time stood still. People began to whisper and point fingers towards me as he spoke. I remember being so angry that I marched straight to the altar, as my father was proudly heading back to his seat, to let the entire church have a piece of my mind. Of course, the church loved this scandal. After that night, my mother and I became the hot topic of gossip in our church community. I had to sit through sermons that were preached against me and my mother on how we out to treat our husbands and parents. My father never apologized or put an end to the gossip. I was so humiliated that I stopped attending church all together.

After one year of not attending church, I had an encounter with a witch who pretended to be a Christian, only to try to sell my soul. That encounter with a witch, led me running back to Christ. I will explain more in depth, in the next chapter. I started attending a new church, faithfully. I was active and on fire for the Lord. After being a member for about one year, that all changed. During a "Hallelujah Night" the Youth Pastor of the church, made illicit comments to me. The first time it happened, I thought my mind was playing tricks on me. I didn't know everything in the bible, but I knew adultery is a sin. I was so heartbroken, because I really loved the church, and I didn't know who I could trust to share what happened. Who would believe the new girl over the prominent pastor? So, I told only one friend whom I'd invited to ministry with me and soon after I left the ministry all together. One year later, it was reported that this same Youth Pastor, impregnated a youth member. For a long time, I carried guilt and shame for not speaking up. Although, I didn't tell the elders of the church, GOD fought my battles and exposed the pastor.

After that incident, I told GOD that I would give church another chance. I started attending a new church, my third. I was actively involved. I learned so much about spiritual warfare, fasting and prayer. I attended that church for about three years. I had joined the children's ministry and loved it. One day, the leader left the ministry, for personal reasons and a few weeks later, without warning they removed most or all who were under her leadership. I was so heartbroken because I was stripped from serving the Lord when I had done nothing wrong. I also witnessed other leaders be removed from serving without doing anything wrong. What hurt most was that after I shared my personal testimony in the church and asked for prayer. Many gossiped about my situation rather than praying for my deliverance. I experienced public ridicule from certain leaders. I also experienced being sexually assaulted by a man who asked me for a ride home. After repeated hurts, I left the ministry and I never saw church the same.

How did "*Church Hurt*" affect my life?

I would spend the next few years spiritually unsettled. I became very critical and suspicious of others in the Body of Christ, especially male preachers. I jumped from church to church, avoiding commitment. I would be the last to attend church service and the first one to leave after the sermon is preached to avoid all fellowship with believers. I avoided sharing my testimony or vulnerability with others. I didn't believe that I was worthy of being loved and accepted by the Church, so I walked around with a cloud of Betrayal.

> *I jumped from church to church, avoiding commitment. I would be the last to attend church service and the first one to leave after the sermon is preached to avoid all fellowship with believers.*

How did I RISE from Church Hurt?

The antidote for *Church Hurt* is *Forgiveness*.

During the pandemic, I experienced the presence of GOD on a new level. I found myself spending hours in worship and studying the word of GOD. It was in the presence of GOD, that I discovered the root of my church hurt. It was also in the presence of GOD, at my present church ministry, that I found deliverance. I was bound, until JESUS Christ set me free. Forgiveness is the key to true FREEDOM. I had to forgive those who publicly humiliated me, scorned me, gossiped about me, and defamed my character. I had to forgive my parents who tried to publicly humiliate me. I had to forgive the minister who preached a sermon on me. I had to forgive the youth pastor who tried to take advantage of me. I had to forgive the men who professed Christ but violated me. And most importantly, I had to forgive myself for the role that I played in all of this. Through Christ JESUS, I phenomenally ROSE from "Church Hurt" back to rightful position as the Bride of Christ.

🌹 ENCOURAGEMENT 🌹

There is no perfect church. The church is like a hospital, designed to heal those who are sick. You will find healed and unhealed people in church ministry. We all need a dose of: Faith, Hope, and Love. We must place our confidence in GOD. People may fail us, but GOD will never fail. It is time to forgive those from the pulpit and pews who hurt us. May we find the courage to forgive, grow and continue to walk in love towards the Body of Christ.

AFFIRMATIONS:
1. I extend love to others, as Christ JESUS loves me.
2. I release the past.
3. I forgive those who have wronged me.

Bible verses to help **OVERCOME** Church Hurt:
1. "By this all will know that you are My disciples, if You have love for another."
   - John 13:35
2. Proverbs 6: 16-19 "Let no corrupting talk come out of your mouths, but only such as is good for building up, as fits the occasion, that it may give grace to those who hear.

3. Exodus 23:1 "You shall not spread false reports. You shall not join hands with a wicked man to be malicious."
4. Matthew 7: 1-2: Do not judge, or you too will be judged. For in the same way, you judge others, you will be judged, and with measure you use, it will be measured to you."
5. Matthew 18: 15 "If your brother or sister sins, go and point out their fault, just between the two of you. If they listen to you, you have won them over."

PRAYER:

Dear: Heavenly Father,

I come before your throne of grace, and I ask for your forgiveness from all hidden sin of unforgiveness in my heart. I asked for your help, through the Holy Spirit, to forgive all pastors, leaders from the fivefold ministry, and church members who have ever hurt me. Help me to let the offenses go. Help me to walk in Love. May I RISE this day from Church Hurt back to the untainted BRIDE of Christ, in JESUS mighty name, I pray. Amen.

Phenomenally She Rose: *Marjorie Rose Bernadin*

Chapter 5:

She *ROSE* from ~~Depression~~

"Now faith is the substance of things hoped for,
the evidence of things not seen"
- Hebrew 11:1

POEM: Set *Free* by the Living Word 🌷
Written by: Marjorie Rose Bernadin

Fear, what have you to do with me.
You have overtaken my mother and her mother and are now in pursuit of me.
Terror, in the shadow of the night.
Overwhelmed with guilt of yesterday,
Dread of tomorrow.
Restlessness amid today.
Labeled as Anxiety.

Double mindedness, what have you to do with me.
Your hesitance stands amidst my breakthrough,
In you, my identity has been questioned,
Repeated vicious cycles of redundancy,
Years of movement without clarity.
Consumed by wavelength of highs and lows.
Labeled as Bi-polar.

Gloom, what have you to do with me,
A life consumed with clouds of heaviness,
Hopelessness, as my only companion,
Attempts to take the very life, not owned.
Surface smiles, conjure against the pain of my yesterday.
Labeled as Depression.

To be labeled as depressed, anxious, bipolar, fearful, doubtful

and in despair,
Was just the beginning of a rooted character formation.
Till an encounter with the living WORD set me free.
John 1:1-2, "In the beginning was the word,
And the word was with GOD, and the Word was GOD.
He was with GOD in the beginning."
Amid mental health crisis,
The living WORD spoke.
It said, "No weapon formed against me shall be able to prosper.
I am the head and not the tail, above and not beneath."
I am healed and I am restored.
The living WORD spoke.
"GOD has not given you a spirit of fear, but of
power, love, and of a sound mind.
I can do all things through Christ who strengthens me."

The living WORD spoke.
The living WORD breath life unto me,
The WORD washed away my fears and doubts,
The WORD gave me an identity.
Mind renewed,
Life transform,
What once bonded me, has released me.
In the presence of the living WORD, I am set free.
We overcame by the blood of the lamb.
and the WORD of our testimony,
who the SON sets free,
is FREE indeed.

"HOPE is the oil that ignites the manifestation of our FAITH"

-Marjorie Rose Bernadin

"**DISCLAIMER:** *Mental Health is a very sensitive topic that needs to be addressed. Everything written in this book is based on my personal life experiences. I am not licensed to provide any medical advice. If you or someone that you know currently battles with thoughts of harming yourself or others, seek medical and professional support, immediately. At the end of this chapter, I will provide a list of national Hotlines that you may contact for further assistance.*"

Depression:

For one to be whole, the Mind, Body, Soul, and Spirit must align. For years, my mental state was consumed with Anxiety, Depression, Doubt and Fear. Overwhelmed by guilt of yesterday, dread of tomorrow, and restlessness of my today. I didn't know that I could be set free until I renewed my mind with the Living Word. To HOPE in what you cannot see, opens the doors to Possibilities and shuts the door to despair. I Phenomenally *ROSE* into wholeness, through HOPE in JESUS Christ.

Since I was a young child, I struggled with sadness. I walked around with a spirit of heaviness because I felt rejected. I didn't believe that I was valuable enough, pretty enough, smart enough or good enough to be loved and accepted. My lack of self-worth and the abuse from childhood led to years of depression and suicidal ideation. I had repeated thoughts of cutting my wrist. At the age of 16, I attempted suicide by taking pills.

One day, during high school, I called one of my older sisters for help. I begged her to save me. She drove five hours with her husband to come check on me. That weekend was when my mother discovered the intensity of my mental state. My mother witnessed one of my siblings attempt suicide a few years prior, so she didn't take it likely. She smelled my breath and removed all deadly chemicals from the home. She went outside and screamed and cried for a few hours. My parents didn't believe in therapy, so instead they just prayed for me. While everyone was focused on my physical state, it was my mind and soul that were broken.

At age 18, after my first heartbreak, I planned meticulously how to crash my car on the highway to make it seem like an accident. Thank GOD, for stopping my plans. I was tormented by the thoughts of death. I carried with me guilt, shame, unforgiveness, worthlessness, and rejection. For years, I cried myself to sleep. I once prayed and begged GOD to take my life because I feared that if I committed suicide, I'd be in hell. I didn't want to live because I didn't see a reason to live. I was Hopeless.

How did "DEPRESSION" affect my life?

Depression caused me to live a life of hopelessness. Depression caused me to attempt suicide as a teen and young adult. Depression caused me to turn to alcohol to numb my pain. For years, I cried myself to sleep. I prayed for GOD to take my life and put an end to my misery. Depression caused me to make careless decisions and risky behaviors. Depression led to my anger and bitterness. I treated others harshly because misery loves company. Depression led me to operate with a victim mentality, looking for others to save me. Connecting to trauma bonding relationships seeking for someone to love me. A repeated vicious cycle of misery.

> *Depression led to my anger and bitterness. I treated others harshly because misery loves company. Depression led me to operate with a victim mentality, looking for others to save me.*

How did I RISE from DEPRESSION:
The antidote to Depression is HOPE.

At the age of 35, I am blessed to be alive. I am here to testify, that abundant life through Christ JESUS is possible. I had to go through years of counseling, deliverance and had to renew my mind with the Word of GOD. I had to monitor and journal my thoughts. I also created affirmations and declarations for JOY. Most importantly, I had to decide that I was going to be "HAPPY" no matter my circumstance. I surrounded myself with people, places and things that made me Happy. One of my places of serenity is at the beach. I also completed a 90-day journey of healing: Body, Mind, Soul, and Spirit. During that time, I vested in eating healthy, exercising, prayer, deliverance at church, journaling, forgiveness, therapy, and self-care routines. Now, I am the happiest ever been. I am joyful. I am living the abundant life that Christ JESUS paid, to set me free. Through JESUS Christ, I Phenomenally ROSE from Depression back to Hopefulness.

🌹 ENCOURAGEMENT 🌹

JESUS came to heal the brokenhearted. JESUS came to comfort all who mourn. JESUS came to give beauty for ashes, oil of joy for mourning. JESUS came to proclaim the acceptable year of the LORD. JESUS came to set the captives free.

Suffering from a Mental Health disorder does not mean that your life is over. GOD healed and delivered me from Depression. GOD desires to heal you from all Mental Disorders. The devil wants to steal, kill, and destroy destinies. But JESUS Christ came to set captives free and to give life more abundantly.

I held firm to the promises of GOD, that by HIS stripes I am healed: physically, mentally, emotionally, spiritually, and relationally. Choose to forgive, this day. Learn to let go of any thoughts that produce sadness, worry, doubt, guilt, shame, and fear. You must have faith and meditate on GOD's scriptures. Peace and Joy are your birthright. May you Phenomenally RISE from whatever Mental Disorder you faced, into a place of Hopefulness.

AFFIRMATIONS:
1. I am full of JOY in the Lord always.
2. My past is forgiven by GOD.
3. Each day is an opportunity for me to HOPE again and embrace GOD's newness.
4. My life is worth living.

Scriptures to **OVERCOME** Depression:

1. "Now faith is the substance of things hoped for, the evidence of things not seen." (Hebrew 11:1).
2. Casting all your anxieties on him because he cares for you" (1 Peter 5:7).
3. "The Lord is near to the brokenhearted and saves the crushed in spirit" (Psalm 34:18).
4. "The Spirit of the Lord GOD is upon Me, because the LORD has anointed Me to preach good tidings to the poor. He has sent Me to heal the brokenhearted, to proclaim liberty to the captives, and the opening of the prison to those who are bound." (Isaiah 61:1)
5. "Do not sorrow, for the joy of the LORD is your strength" (Nehemiah 8:10b)

PRAYER:

Dear: Heavenly Father,

I come before your throne of grace, and I ask for your forgiveness of sins. Sorry for allowing sadness to take root in my life. Forgive me for dwelling on thoughts of sadness, fear, guilt, shame, and doubt. Forgive me for any past attempts to take my own life. My life does not belong to me; therefore, I have no right to take it away. I asked for your help, through the Holy Spirit to meditate on scriptures of Hope and Joy. Help me to believe that life is worth living. Help me to see the good in every circumstance. May you comfort me and heal my broken heartedness. I pray that Peace and Joy are my birthright. May I RISE this day from Depression into the place of Hopefulness in JESUS mighty name, I pray, amen.

Phenomenally She Rose: *Marjorie Rose Bernadin*

Phenomenally She Rose: *Marjorie Rose Bernadin*

Chapter 6:

She *ROSE* from Witchcraft

"Let no one be found among you who sacrifices their son or daughter in the fire, who practices divination or sorcery, interprets omens, engages in witchcraft, or cast spells, or who is a medium or spiritist or who consults the dead. anyone who does these things is detestable practices the LORD your GOD will drive out those nations before you" – Deuteronomy 18: 10-12

POEM: **Generational Curse BREAKER** 🌷
Written by: Marjorie Rose Bernadin

They danced and they drummed to the rhythm of ceremonial Dances.
Voodou practitioners led praises to the ancient gods,
Lwa of Damballa, Dan Petro, Dan Wedo, Congo, and Baron Samedi.
Sacrifices made of the young and old,
Haitian roots dated back to Africa,
My ancestors worshipped Loa Damballa, ancient African Serpent god.
They whispered for me, they visited me,
To continue with deep rooted traditions.
But they could not find me, for I was set apart.

Chosen by GOD, to tear down the very walls that my ancestors Built.
Yes, I was predestined by Christ JESUS,
Covered by blood, to renounce old covenants,
To tear down evil altars,
To break generational curses,
To create generational blessings and
Produce godly offspring.
I, and my descendants are one, in a new blood covenant.
My ancestors worshiped the dead,
But I worship the ONE true living GOD, Elohim.
I am the generational curse breaker in my lineage.

Phenomenally She Rose: *Marjorie Rose Bernadin*

"A Saved Christian without Deliverance Remains Oppressed"
-Marjorie Rose Bernadin

Born in North America, rooted in Haiti, traced back to Africa, the mother continent. I am of Haitian descent, with roots sturdy enough to build fortified walls against slavery. Roots that built branches in me that are immovable against the currents of life. Haiti, the first independent black republic in the world. Roots with tastes buds for diri (rice), tasso (steak bites, beef bites), banan peze (pressed plantain), legume (stew). Roots with robust sound for Kompa music. Roots of folklore ceremonials to ancient Lao (deites). Haiti (Ayiti) is my ancestors beloved homeland.

Bloodline:
It was during my college years that I'd discovered the tracing to my maternal heritage. Long before my birth, witchcraft and human blood sacrifice was prevalent. Long before my birth was a lineage of those who worshipped Loa Damballa, ancient African serpent god. Voodoo was a part of my ancestor's culture. As a child, I would have dreams and visions of being surrounded by snakes, each night. It was at the tender age of seven, that I accepted JESUS Christ as my Lord and Savior and that was the first time that the dreams of snakes faded away.

Witchcraft:
In 2006, I had an encounter with a witch that would forever change the trajectory of my life. I drove to a nearby gas station in

Phenomenally She Rose: *Marjorie Rose Bernadin*

Miami Gardens, Florida. Upon paying, a woman followed me outside and began fortune telling. She began to tell me about my life, struggles and heartbreak. At first, I was very hesitant; but she reassured me that she was a Christian sent by GOD to help me. She convinced me to allow her to pray for me. She held my hands and spoke a prayer; the rest was history. She prayed in a strange language that I perceived to be tongues. Her prayer led me under a trance. She asked me for $300 to be exact and I immediately went to a nearby ATM to withdraw money and drove to my house for the rest. I drove back to the gas station and gave her $300. She assured me that the elders would burn candles. We exchanged telephone contacts. The very next day, she called me to meet her at her house to complete the process. Without notifying anyone, I left.

    Upon arrival, she traced a cross on my forehead, marked with oil. She had me walk to the nearest gas station to buy specifics: one carton of eggs and one paper towel. She requested more money. I did exactly as I was told, no questions and no hesitation. She led me to a room, lit with candles everywhere. She prayed for me, all over my body. She rubbed my stomach with an egg then cracked the egg on a book, maybe a bible. That's when I awoke from the trance. Afraid for my life, I wept. I didn't tell anyone of my whereabouts. She insisted that we head to the cemetery that very day, to bury what was in the egg. I cried and cried, hysterically. But there was no one to save me. I pleaded with her to bury the egg in her backyard; but she impatiently insisted we go to the cemetery. That is when I began to pray in my heart, and I asked GOD to save and deliver me. It was then that I heard a voice say to me, "Tell her that you need to go to work". I just obeyed. Told

Phenomenally She Rose: *Marjorie Rose Bernadin*

her that I needed to go to work. With fury, she insisted that we complete the burial at the cemetery. I prayed for GOD to help me.

Then something shifted. She agreed. She provided me with a handful of colorful rocks, wrapped in aluminum foil.

She instructed me that when I arrived home, place the rocks in the tub, fill my tub halfway with water and lay in the tub for about five minutes. She said once I did it,

> *She instructed me that when I arrived home, place the rocks in the tub, fill my tub halfway with water and lay in the tub for about five minutes. She said once I did it, everything would be fine.*

everything would be fine. As soon as she allowed me to leave, I fled to my car, parked near the main road, and wept. I cried out to GOD with a heart of repentance because I knew something horrible happened. While parked in my car, I heard a voice tell me, "Don't do what she said." I obeyed.

When I arrived home, I left the rocks, and I got ready for work. At the end of my shift, I heard a voice instruct me to tell my mother everything that happened that day. I did, as instructed. I got home and woke my mother up and told her about my strange encounter. To my astonishment, my mother didn't kill me or disowned me. Instead, she prayed for me and took olive oil and poured it over my body. She prayed against the rocks and threw them outside. She sent me to my room to pray, repent and read the book of psalm. I thought I was free from the Woman that I had met at the gas station. But I was wrong because the woman I met was a witch.

Because of my mother's heritage, she understood what had happened to me. About one year later, GOD revealed through a prophet, that this woman tried to sell my soul. The egg represented me. Had I gone to the cemetery, it would have been my burial. The prophet told me the reason that I didn't die was because the LORD said that I was innocent.

How did "Witchcraft" affect my life?

Witchcraft afflicted my life in so many ways. Following that incident, I spent over 10 years experiencing sickness, lack, failure, and mental attacks. I was diagnosed with several illnesses. My illnesses were related to my stomach, blood, thyroid, and womb. In 2007, I had abdominal surgery to remove my gallbladder. Afterwards, I'd developed irritable bowel syndrome. I spent years having chronic diarrhea. I spent a few years not being able to control my bowels. Many times, throughout the years, I toileted on myself because I didn't make it to the restroom on time. I went from a size extra-large to extra small. Because of my drastic weight loss, many shared concerns about my health. I met a classmate at a restaurant, who was shocked to see my weight and he asked if I was dying, in front of guests. I went home and wept.

For years, I lived a life afflicted with lack, failure, sickness, mental attacks, and barrenness. I couldn't keep a steady job, money, relationship and was kicked out of my ASN nursing program. I was so ashamed of my new weight because I didn't look healthy. I went through a season feeling as though GOD was punishing me. I requested for GOD to take away the burden; yet HE replied, "My GRACE is sufficient." Over the years, no matter what private or public battles I faced, I kept my faith in JESUS Christ.

How did I RISE from Witchcraft?

The antidote for **Witchcraft** is *Total Deliverance* and a lifestyle of *Sanctification.*

Salvation and Deliverance are not one of the same. A person may be saved but still oppressed and bound by unclean spirits. To accept JESUS Christ as Lord and Savior is an assurance to eternal life. Deliverance is a process that requires repentance, renunciation, breaking of soul ties and a life of sanctification. Although I was saved, I needed to go through the PROCESS of deliverance.

> *Deliverance is a process that requires repentance, renunciation, breaking of soul ties and a life of sanctification. Although I was saved, I needed to go through the PROCESS of deliverance.*

Deliverance requires a sanctified life. Although, I am in this world, I am not of this world. I had to separate myself from certain music, movies, places, and conversations. I prayed. I fasted. I forgave. I plead the blood of JESUS over me and my family daily. I attended a few deliverance services. I watched a lot of prophetic prayers online. I renounce witchcraft from my bloodline. I prayed against evil altars built by my ancestors to be torn down. I renounce any hidden sins in my life. I meditated and prayed on scriptures concerning witchcraft. I lived a consecrated life, to the best of my abilities. Through Christ JESUS, I ROSE from Witchcraft into *Total Deliverance*, through the process of *Sanctification*.

🌷 ENCOURAGEMENT 🌷

Witchcraft is an act of manipulation and a state of rebellion. Occult powers are evil alongside white magic, black magic, tarot card reading, Ouija boards, and astrology. Leviticus 19:31 states, "Give no regards to medium and familiar spirits; do not seek after them, to be defiled by them. I am the LORD your God."

May you also use discernment before you allow anyone to lay hands or pray for you. Many witches and wizards have masqueraded as holy vessels amongst the Body of Christ, to steal, kill and destroy destinies.

If you have been a victim of witchcraft, you must repent of your sins, accept JESUS Christ as Lord and Savior, renounce sin, and live a consecrated life. GOD is mighty to deliver you. GOD is POWERFUL enough to save you, to protect you and to keep you safe from evil. You do not need to turn to psychics, witches, wizards, horoscopes, familiar spirits, egg wash, crystals, wands, chants, sage, or voodoo ceremonials to protect you. GOD is mighty to save.

AFFIRMATION:
1. *I am redeemed by the Blood of the LAMB*
2. *I am set free from Witchcraft through Christ JESUS.*
3. *I recover all that the enemy stole from me.*

Bible verses to help OVERCOME Witchcraft:
1. "But the cowardly, the unbelieving, the vile, the murderers, the sexually immoral, those who practice magic arts, the idolaters and all liars- their place will be in the fiery lake of burning sulfur. This is the second death." (Revelation 21:8)

2. "Let no one be found among you who sacrifices their son or daughter in the fire, who practices divination or sorcery, interprets omens, engages in witchcraft, or cast spells, or who is a medium or spiritist or who consults the dead. Anyone who does these things is detestable practices the LORD your GOD will drive out those nations before you" (Deuteronomy 18: 10-12)

PRAYER

Dear: Heavenly Father,

I come before your throne of grace. I ask for your forgiveness of all sin. I ask you to forgive me for any act of witchcraft done by myself or those from my heritage. I renounce witchcraft, black magic, white magic, psychic readings, horoscopes, consulting the dead or familiar spirits, egg wash, crystals, chants, sage, and voodoo ceremonials. May I RISE this day from Witchcraft into the place of deliverance and continuous lifestyle of Sanctification, in JESUS mighty name, I pray, amen.

Phenomenally She Rose: *Marjorie Rose Bernadin*

Chapter 7:

She *ROSE* from Death

"Most assuredly, I say to you, he who hears My word and Believes in Him who sent Me has everlasting life, and shall not come into judgement, but has passed from death into life" – John 5:24

POEM: **Lamb of GOD who ROSE** 🌹
Written by: Marjorie Rose Bernadin

Lamb of GOD who takes away the sins of this WORLD,
Have mercy on us this day.
You were betrayed with a Kiss,
Abandoned by your Disciples,
Traded for a murderer,
They cried, "Crucify! Crucify!"

Wounded for our transgressions,
Crushed for our iniquities,
Pierced on every side,
Mocked by your own kind,
Given vinegar for thirst.
Punishment for being a SON,
They cried, "Crucify! Crucify!"

You became the ultimate Sacrifice,
Holy and Acceptable,
You carried the SINS of this world,
Cursed, as you hung on a tree.
Becoming detestable to Abba Father.
You cried, "Eli, Eli, lama sabachthani?"
That is, "My God, My God, why have
You forsaken me?"
Yielding your spirit, you died.

They celebrated because you were crucified.
Not knowing that was the Ultimate will of the Father,
For you to DIE.
The tomb was guarded, soldiers on every side.
But on the THIRD day, prophecy would be fulfilled.
The SAVIOR would RISE.
Carrying VICTORY in your wings.
Whoever believes in you would not perish but have
Everlasting life.
Because you ROSE from the grave,
I and my descendants shall RISE…

"A seed halfway planted cannot GROW effectively."
-Marjorie Rose Bernadin

You cannot RISE without knowing the one who first ROSE, Jesus Christ. There are so many depictions in the Holy Bible that demonstrates the RISING of our Lord and Savior.

Jesus ROSE from Controversy. He was placed in the womb of Mary, a woman not yet married, carrying a child of promise by the Holy Spirit, in an era that stoned women if they were not pure or virgins (Matthew 1: 18-25).

Jesus ROSE from Child Massacre. His family fled to Egypt to escape the killings of innocent children, led by King Herod (Matthew 2: 16-18).

Jesus ROSE from temptation. His ministry began at 30 years of age. Baptized by John, then led to the wilderness for training. 40 days and 40 nights, he fasted. Tempted by Satan in every way. Weak in body yet filled by the Holy Spirit. He overcame every temptation with… "It is written."
(Matthew 4:1-11).

Jesus ROSE from treachery. Betrayed by a kiss, from one who studied him during three years of ministry, Judas (Matthew 26: 47-56).

Lastly, Jesus ROSE from the dead. Wounded for our transgressions, crushed for our iniquities, pierced on every side, mocked by HIS own kind, given vinegar for thirst. Hung on a tree, as a curse. Detestable to Abba Father, for He carried the sins of the world. Punishment for being a SON was death by crucifixion. Buried in the tomb, but on the third day, prophecy would be fulfilled. The Savior and King has RISEN. Because He ROSE, all who believes in JESUS shall RISE again (Matthew 28:1-10).

How did JESUS Christ RISE?

To RISE we must first be Buried. A seed halfway planted cannot grow effectively. Many of us have unburied past traumatic experiences related to rejection, heartbreak, low self-esteem, church hurt, mental health disorders, or witchcraft. Our lens has tainted our identity. Poorly soil, has led us to becoming lukewarm, half healed, still broken vessels, barely breathing. GOD desires us to be healed and whole. To sprout into something NEW, the old seed must die.

> *To RISE we must first be Buried. A seed halfway planted cannot grow effectively.*

NO longer will we remain on the surface. It's time for a burial. Death must take place before the resurrection. Death to the old life. Death to old patterns. Death to addictions. Death to hurts. Death to pain. Death to traumas of our yesterday. Death to unresolved issues. Death to old dreams that were not align with the will of our Heavenly Father. Death to unhealthy emotions. Death to a tainted identity. Death to sin.

🌹 ENCOURAGEMENT 🌹

Those experiences that we faced in life, were the trials needed to OVERCOME into Triumphant. Those experiences helped to develop our character into the ROSE that we are called to be. A seed once buried in pain, hurt, betrayals, abuse, low self-worth, sickness, failure, and a brokenness has now sprouted into a lovely flower. A *ROSE* filled with love, joy, peace, patience, kindness, goodness, faithfulness, gentleness, and self-control. A blossoming Rose.

It doesn't matter who rejected you, GOD affirms you.

It does not matter who broke your heart, GOD can restore you.

It does not matter how many mistakes you have made; GOD values you.

It doesn't matter if you hated your size, height, or appearance. GOD calls you fearfully and wonderfully made.

It doesn't matter if you have battled with mental health disorders, GOD can heal you.

It doesn't matter if you were a victim of witchcraft attacks, GOD can deliver you.

The only thing that matters is that GOD truly loves you and nothing can separate you from the Love of GOD.

AFFIRMATION:
1. I am Loved by GOD.
2. I am Healed.
3. I am Restored.
4. I am Triumphant.
5. I am Resurrected from death to Life.

PRAYER for Repentance and Salvation (Pray out loud)

Dear Heavenly Father, I come before your throne of grace, asking for your forgiveness of sin. Forgive me for holding on to dead things and unfruitful things in my life such as: rejection, hurt, heart brokenness, depression, unforgiveness, bitterness, failures, disappointments, abuse, and addictions. Today, I choose to let go and allow you to create in me a clean heart and renew your right spirit within me. I choose to forgive all who have hurt me, abused me, and abandoned me. I acknowledge that I am a sinner, in need of a Savior. I believe that JESUS Christ is Lord and Savior. JESUS died and rose on the third day. Through faith in Christ Jesus, I shall resurrect from death to eternal Life. May JESUS Christ be my Lord and Savior this day and forevermore. May you forgive me of all sins and write my name into the LAMB's Book of Life. Phenomenally may I RISE from all dead things, back to Abundant Life, through JESUS Christ, amen.

Bible verses to help OVERCOME obstacles:

1. "GOD is within her; she will not fall" (Psalm 46:5)
2. Then He took the child by the hand, and said to her, "Talitha, Cumi," which is translated, "Little girl, I say to you, arise." (Mark 5:41)
3. I can do all things through Christ who strengthens me" (Philippians 4:13)
4. "Blessed is the man who endures temptation; for when he has been approved, he will receive the crown of life which the Lord has promised to those who love Him" (James 1:12)

5. Have I not commanded you? Be strong and of good courage; do not be afraid, nor be dismayed, for the LORD your God is with you wherever you go." (Joshua 1:9)

Phenomenally She Rose: *Marjorie Rose Bernadin*

ABOUT THE AUTHOR

Marjorie Rose Bernadin a woman of faith and substance. She is a businesswoman, real estate agent, nurse, poet, future bestselling author, and speaker. She is the founder of Phenomenally She ROSE ministry, a platform dedicated to empowering women, of all ages and background, to RISE from all Trials of life into a Triumphant living, through faith in Christ Jesus. Phenomenally She ROSE ministry aims to provides women with resources to food donation, workshops, career placement and mental health awareness.

Marjorie enjoys traveling, cruising, dining, cooking, creative writing, going to the beach and anything relating to the Arts. She currently resides in South Florida, alongside her dog, Marvel. She hopes to one day share her beautiful life with her future husband and children.

Phenomenally She Rose: *Marjorie Rose Bernadin*

Marjorie Rose Celebration

Phenomenally She Rose: *Marjorie Rose Bernadin*

Phenomenally She Rose: *Marjorie Rose Bernadin*

Phenomenally She Rose: *Marjorie Rose Bernadin*

You don't want to miss this conference.

Phenomenally She Rose: *Marjorie Rose Bernadin*

MENTAL HEALTH RESOURCES

Mental Health Hotline
988 Mental Health Chat - 988 Suicide & Crisis Lifeline
https://www.988lifeline.org

---

988 Lifeline provides 24/7, free and confidential crisis resources for you and loved ones. Anxious? Depressed? Text 988 for to chat with a trained crisis counselor for free.

National Mental Health Hotline | 866-903-3787

https://mentalhealthhotline.org

The Mental Health Hotline is a **free, confidential 24-hour hotline** for anyone struggling with depression, anxiety, or any mental health crisis.

Crisis Text Line | Text HOME To 741741 free, 24/7 Crisis ...

Crisis Text Line
https://www.crisistextline.org

Crisis Text Line provides free, 24/7 support via text message. We're here for everything: anxiety, depression, suicide, school. Text HOME to 741741.

Phenomenally She Rose: *Marjorie Rose Bernadin*

Phenomenally She Rose: *Marjorie Rose Bernadin*

Phenomenally She Rose: *Marjorie Rose Bernadin*

Phenomenally She Rose: *Marjorie Rose Bernadin*

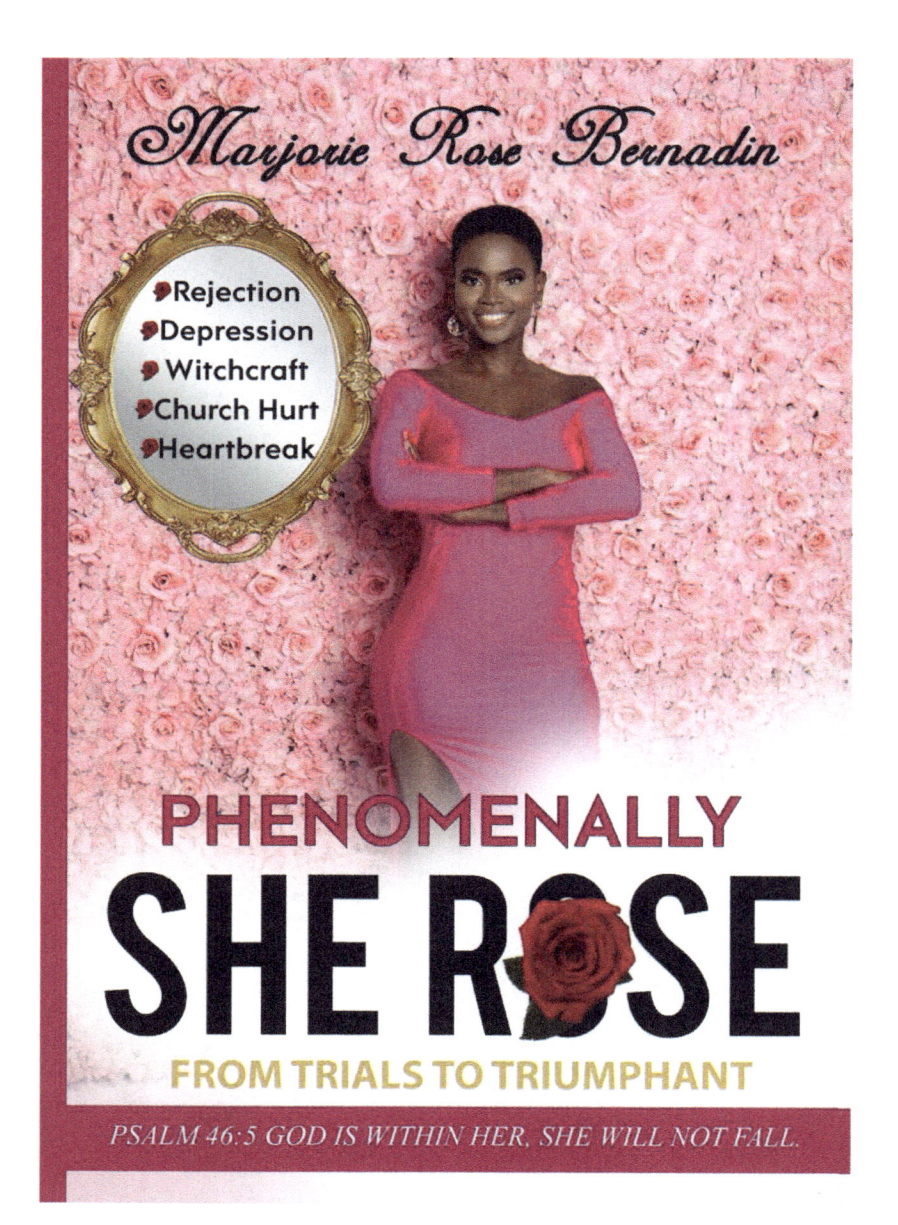

Marjorie Rose Bernadin

- Rejection
- Depression
- Witchcraft
- Church Hurt
- Heartbreak

PHENOMENALLY SHE ROSE

FROM TRIALS TO TRIUMPHANT

PSALM 46:5 GOD IS WITHIN HER, SHE WILL NOT FALL.

Made in the USA
Columbia, SC
31 May 2023